MW00940277

REST IN GOD
How To Keep Living When Life Gets Hard

CHERYLE T RICKS

Xulon Press

Xulon Press
2301 Lucien Way #415
Maitland, FL 32751
407.339.4217
www.xulonpress.com

Printed in the United States of America.

ISBN-13: 978-1-5456-7664-6

To: 700 Club,
With God we can
get through anything!!

Love
Cheryle T. Ricks
443-447-7267

Endorsements

To God be the glory! Ms. Ricks has shared with us her personal journey in a very vivid and meaningful way. She did not sugar coat or camouflage her struggles, nor did she leave us with doubts about what faith in God can do, when we trust Him. This book is encouraging, and it is also the road map of a very strong Christian woman shining a light for others to follow. I am sure others would agree after reading this book, when I say that we are very proud of Ms. Ricks for touching and inspiring us to never give up or give in when God is in the equation. Thank you, Cheryle!

—Chaplain Samuel L. Smith

This book is a step-by-step guide that will allow any person to see the good in their life in spite of the problems that show up in it. The author makes it very clear that a relationship with God is essential if you want to enjoy life when the storms come. It is very easy to read, and it will keep you turning the pages. After reading this book, you will surely know more about who God is and how much He loves all of us!

—Carolyn Johnson

This book is a how-to manual that shows the importance of nurturing a relationship with Jehovah God-in-three persons by praise and giving thanks in everything. It encourages one to magnify the name of Jehovah the Sovereign God instead of the "troubles" one may face and to look for the blessings in the midst of challenges; since all things are working together for the good of them who love Jehovah GOD, the Lord, and are called according to His purpose.

—Cheryl Ann Scott

DEDICATION AND ACKNOWLEDGMENTS

I dedicate this book to my Lord and Savior, Jesus Christ who gave me His love, His grace, His mercy, and His strength to endure, overcome, and thrive on this journey called life.

To my family: Lorraine Lifsey, Lynda Thomason, Frances Mealy, Joseph James Mealy, Jr., and Pamela Mealy, thank you all for never allowing me to be alone! I thank God that you are my family!

To my sister, Marguerite Hudson and my brother-in-law, Herbert Hudson, thank you for opening up your home to me, supporting, and encouraging me to reach for my dreams. Without you, I would not have been able to finish writing this book. I am forever grateful to both of you for all you have done for me!

To my mother: Marguerite Edna Spicer Mealy who showed me the unconditional love of a mother and believed that I could become the woman I am today. Mom, I will always be grateful for your prayers and your faith in me. I feel your presence every day. Mothers truly do come in handy.

To my father: Joseph James Mealy, Sr. who taught me how to help others, to be unselfish, to slow down and look at what I was doing. Those lessons continue to serve me after all these years.

To my sons: Ronald Cowan, Jr. and Larry Tyrone Ricks, Jr., thank you for being the strong towers who keep our family standing. Thank you for allowing God to help you both to overcome the pain I caused you when you were young boys. Time heals all wounds when we give the pain to God and allow Him to show us how that pain creates the person we ultimately become because of it. I am proud of the men you have become!

To my daughters: Chevelle Ricks and Sherelle Ricks Witherspoon, thank you for helping me to grow into a twenty-first century woman. I have learned so much from each of you. I am proud of the women you have become!

To my grandsons: Kasshan L. Cowan, Diontay Braheem Ricks, Derek Defontaine Goldsmith, Larry T. Ricks, III, Malik Jauan Hargis, and Cortly Witherspoon, Jr., thank you for growing into the rocks that will build the future generations in our family. I am proud of each of you!

To my only granddaughter: Aniya Satea Whitfield, thank you for being so amazing. You are beautiful and very talented. You will empower our future generations to become all that they can be. I am very proud of you!

To my dearest friend: Francis Charles Snyder, thank you for helping me see my true beauty and for all of your support and confidence in me. I thank God for what you bring to my life!

To my daughter-in-law Lisa Jones Ricks and my son-in-law Cortly Witherspoon, Sr., thank you both for all you add to our family. I love and appreciate both of you for making our family even more special!

To my literary team: Marguerite Hudson, Attorney Cheryl Ann Scott, Deacon Austin L. Patterson, Marie Minor, and Chaplain Samuel L. Smith, thank you all for the feedback, encouragement, guidance, help, and support I needed to finish writing this book. I am forever grateful to all of you!

To my amazing village of strength:

Catherine Dixon-Kheir; Joi Ford; Marguerite Hudson; Sherelle Ricks Witherspoon; Chevelle Ricks; Larry T.

Ricks, Jr.; Ronald Cowan, Jr.; Lorraine Lifsey; Marie Minor; Bishop Matthew E. Bradby, II; Candice Bradby; Bishop Michael Smith; Pastor Barbara Smith; Shelah Zakat; Sisters of Power Of Faith Church in Baltimore, Maryland; Andrew "Brian" Daye Sr.; Carmen Holloway; Olivia Stewart; Jubilee Perry; Bonita White; James Haynes; Valencia Sketers; Janet Hall; Kenneth Morris; Martha Newby; Dackeyia Q. Sterling; Irene Asiama; Pamela Bishop; Dr. Miles Harrison; Dr. Mayer Gorbaty; Dr. Harini Balu; Dr. Sean Gunning; Lauren Houlday, CRNP; Dr. Ginette Braziel; Clement Adebayo, R.ph.; The American Cancer Society; Cancer Care; Cathy Brice Hirsch; Reach to Recovery International; Maria Cheeyou; Attorneys: Cheryl Ann Scott, Owen Jaris, Charlene A. Wilson, Ellyn Riedi, and Richard Lebovitz. Thank you all for the support, assistance, and love each of you gave me when I was going through all of the challenges I shared in this book. I could not have made it through any of it without the role each of you played in my life. I thank God for all of you and the blessing you have been to me!

TABLE OF CONTENTS

FOREWORD
By Deacon Austin L. Patterson

I am very fortunate to have met Cheryle T. Ricks at a business conference in Washington DC, where I was promoting my new business and she was promoting her first book. Little did she know, starting my new business was the result of me making a drastic change in my life due to a sudden debilitating illness that I was determined to overcome. As this book states, "When you're faced with an overwhelming challenge, don't just shut down. Continue to live your best life by praying for God's wisdom, resources, and people to get you through." Talking with her was more of a help to me than I think she even realizes. She is "The One" that God sent my way when I needed to be spiritually uplifted and focused. This book is the epitome of what the Word of God instructs us to do when we go through the challenges of life.

You are never alone in any given situation; this is the message that Cheryle not only professes, but she's a living witness to the guaranteed outcome of putting your trust in the Lord while you're dealing with whatever comes your way. You can't confide in just anyone. Even that needs to be a spirit-led decision, and when the right person is sent to aid you, you'll know.

I want to thank Cheryle for allowing God to use her for that purpose and for being a major factor in going through what has been my greatest life challenge, as she has done for so many others. This book will help anyone who reads it. Absorb the spiritual message it implores you to receive.

Preface:

THE CHERYLE T. RICKS STORY PART TWO

*A*s *I mentioned in my first book,* Sister Circle: The Power Sisterhood- A Guide to Becoming the Woman God Designed You to Be, *life can be very difficult and those difficulties do a work in us like nothing else can. In the first part of my life, I survived domestic violence, a mental health breakdown, and no self-esteem.*

In the second part of my life, I discovered my purpose which is the greatest discovery a person can make. When we learn what we were created to do, we get on the road called Destiny and Purpose. That road is not a journey for the faint of heart! When we step out on faith and pursue the dream and passion that God has put in our heart, we will face trials, tribulations, and challenges that will make us question whether we are doing the right thing.

On my road of Destiny and Purpose, I faced the foreclosure of my home, being diagnosed with skin cancer and breast cancer, being sued by a debt collector, and bankruptcy. But God! God made the worst part of my life the best part of my life. God gave me a true village! During that most difficult time, I learned how many people in my life truly loved and cared about me. It was amazing to see how much love, support, encouragement, assistance, resources, help, hope, and enjoyment my family, friends, and even strangers gave me during the seemingly darkest time of my life.

I continued to live my life in spite of what I was going through. I decided not to make my circumstances my life. I resolved to keep enjoying my life and the people and the things I always had. I reminded myself how blessed I was and how awesome my life still was even though I had these situations. I took everything to God and allowed Him to walk me through those challenges like He had done for every other problem I had faced in my life. I trusted His unconditional love for me and the promises in His Word. I held on to my faith in God, who I was in Him, and the plan He has for my life. I believed He would bring me through everything I was going through and I was going to be the better for having gone through it, and I was!

You see, faith, love, and hope make life and everything else possible! Without these three things, a joy-filled and satisfying life is not obtainable. But more importantly, we must receive the true love of God, keep our faith in Him, and hold on to the hope that God created us for much more than we can see in our current situation. God's Word ensures us that God is able to bring us through, "But Jesus looked at them and said to them, '"With men this is impossible, but with God all things are possible"'(Mat. 19:26, New King James Version).

INTRODUCTION

L ife is full of many ups and downs, trials and tribulations. When our lives are up, we are happy. But,
when our lives are down, we are unhappy and depressed.
I have been going through hardships, difficulties, heart-
aches, and pain my whole life. In my early years, my
situations dictated whether I was going to be happy or
if I was going to be sad, whether I was going to enjoy
my life or whether I felt like life wasn't worth living.
In my middle years, I learned that there was a way to
go through life and have a choice about how my problems, circumstances, or situations would affect how I
enjoyed my life. Today, in spite of having breast cancer
and losing one of my breasts, going through months of
treatment for skin cancer, the foreclosure of my home,
being sued, and filing bankruptcy, I have managed to
live my best life yet. The purpose of this book is to show
you how you too can live your life while living through

some of the most difficult situations a person can face. My faith in God, His love, His Word, His hope, and His promises have allowed me to keep living, loving, and serving my way to my most enjoyable life so far!

No one likes heartache and suffering. However, if you are going through a difficult time right now in your life, I can guarantee four things: One, you are uncomfortable; two, it is painful in some way; three, you are resisting what the situation is creating in you; and, four, you are missing the blessings in the midst of your difficult situation. When we are going through painful places, we don't realize that they are changing us from the inside out. They are also preparing us for blessings that are too amazing to believe. So, come with me on a journey to discover how to enjoy your life while facing the most challenging times of your life.

Chapter One:

PREPARE TO FIGHT

All battles are won or lost based on the posture you take before the fight begins. Before any battle, you must be clear about what you are fighting for and what you hope to win after the battle is over. This takes making a plan and designing your strategy. Once I remembered how much God loved me, I then started thinking about why many people become depressed and suicidal when they are going through the same things that I was facing. I determined that it was because they isolated themselves, they didn't seek help, they looked at their life like it would never get better, or they didn't know that God was able to help them. I also noticed that most people don't want to suffer anything, not even the smallest thing. They don't like to be uncomfortable. They don't want to do without anything. They want what they want when they want it. Life is full of processes, but most people don't like to complete their processes. Many people become overwhelmed by their hardships because they were trying to figure out why they were going through what they were going through. They focus on the crisis or problem, and they allow their problems to overshadow their whole life. I figured out that my life was still good even though I had some bad situations. I decided not to throw away my wonderful life by allowing my situations to overtake the rest of my life.

YOU ARE NOT ALONE

When we are experiencing a difficult time in life, our thoughts tend to run wild. It is important to not believe every thought that crosses your mind. Those thoughts encourage us to isolate ourselves from the very help that God sends us. During our most difficult times, the enemy torments our minds with thoughts of despair and hopelessness. He tries to convince us that the problem we're facing will never change and that every worst possible outcome will happen to us. This could not be further from the truth. Remember that you are not alone. God is always with us, Hebrews 13:5b in the New King James Version (NKJV) of the bible says, "For He Himself has said, "'I will never leave you nor forsake you.'" God will always allow you to feel His presence. Often times, He will send someone to be with us when we're going through the storms of life. The problem, however, is that many of us refuse to acknowledge the people that God sends to walk with us during those difficult times. This is because sometimes the person He sends is a total stranger. I cannot tell you how many strangers God used to help me when I was going through the darkest times in my life. Families are great, but sometimes families are not always the place to find understanding and sympathy because of the long history of past mistakes and immature decisions. Whether God sends a friend, a family member, or a stranger, be open to receiving the blessing God is giving you.

When those life-changing challenges hit my life, my mind started searching for examples I could follow that would allow me to overcome what I was facing. Usually, when we are going through a problem or a crisis, we handle our situations or crisis the same way we see others around us handle theirs. We see people overwhelmed, stressed, and fearful about the same circumstances we are experiencing. Because of this, we believe that there is only one way that we can approach our problem. We don't realize that there can be another way to handle our circumstances. We can do something different. Therefore, I decided not to follow the example of people who had not successfully overcome their situations.

My relationship with God allowed me to decide how I was going to live my life even though I was facing the greatest fight that I have ever encountered. I had to get a grip on my mind. I remembered that there is hope in Christ and that there is no defeat in Him. My anchor in my storm was that God truly, unconditionally loved me! There was nothing that I could do to make Him stop loving me. I could ask God to help me even though I didn't have a perfect performance and had made plenty of mistakes, none of which disqualified me from receiving His help, His mercy, and His blessings! This is what I did to enjoy my life when other people were depressed, stressed, fearful, and emotionally over-whelmed from going through the same situations that I was going through.

LEARN TO GIVE GOD ALL OF
YOUR PROBLEMS

Giving God our problems is one of the greatest priv-ileges we have, next to prayer. When we give every new concern and difficult situation to God, it will allow our problems to become lighter. It also helps us to remain stress free, and it prevents the challenge we are facing from becoming our life. When we let all of our problems pile up, they overwhelms us, which takes our focus off of living, and we begin to worry. When we worry, we stop enjoying our lives and become depressed.

When we understand how much God truly loves us and every other person He has created in the world, we know that He will help us. Our problem in our hands is a burden. Placing our problem in God's hands makes our problem more bearable. God is able to fix, repair, and work out all of our circumstances, so we can have less stress, worry, heartache, frustration, and fear. We must learn to trust that God will give us the victory over the current challenge that we are facing just like He did for all of the other problems we had in the past. This is how we enjoy life and maintain a posture of rest when situations show up in our lives. Learning to keep worry and stress out of your life will allow you to be stable when problems show up. It will not overpower you because you are resting in the care of God.

OUR EMOTIONS PAINT THE
WRONG PICTURE

We must learn to look at our situation without becoming emotional. It will help us see our problem from a more realistic vantage point. Our emotions hinder us from seeing the options that are available to help make things better. When we look at our situations through our emotions, it paints a very dim picture of what we are facing. It hinders us from seeing things in a positive and hopeful way because the emotion we usually see our situation through is fear, and that causes us to become pessimistic about how our situation can be resolved. Fear guides our thoughts, and we start imagining worst case scenarios. We then look for all the ways that our situation or circumstances cannot get better. We tell ourselves that the problem we're facing is the end of our happy lives and our life is no longer worth living. Then depression sets in, and we isolate ourselves from others because we are convinced that no one can help us, which is not true! Others can encourage us and show us how they handled that same problem we are facing. We pray to God about our problems and situations, and God answers our prayers through people. No man is an island unto himself. We all need someone to help us through the maze of life. If we try to live life on our own, life will "eat" us alive!

CHOOSE TO STAY OPPORTUNISTIC
AND EMPOWERED

When life hits you, hold on to your hope. It will make all the difference in your being able to overcome what has shown up in your life. Hope says even though I am going through a difficult situation and I don't know how to fix it, I know that it will get better somehow. Let's face it, how many times in your life have you had a problem, a crisis, a situation, or a circumstance that you didn't know what to do to fix it? How many times have you seen those same problems, situations, and circumstances work out, and you benefited from what you went through? Remembering our past victories and all the things that God has allowed us to overcome will give us the ability to conquer what we are facing right now. When we keep our mind focused on the desired outcome, instead of talking and thinking about our problem all day and all night, we gain great strength. Our thoughts and words then move us into the path of victory. When we allow God to help us with our everyday life, we handle the challenges better because we know that God is leading and guiding us every step of the way. This allows us to remain stable in our uncertain situation.

Chapter Two:

HELP OR HINDRANCE

EVERYONE WILL NOT BE ABLE
TO HELP YOU

One of the greatest challenges we face when we are going through a difficult time is finding someone to help us. So, we reach out to any and everybody looking for some type of help, comfort, and support. We want somebody to understand and help us make sense of it all. We don't want to go through our problem alone. When I was going through the foreclosure of my home, my only thought was save my home. That was the only option I could see. Therefore, I did everything that I could think of. I asked family members, friends, friends of friends, and strangers on Facebook to help me save my home. Then it dawned on me that I never consulted with

God about what He wanted me to do about my house. I soon learned that every person you know cannot walk with you when you are in a difficult place. Everyone will not be able to help you. Everyone does not have faith in God. Therefore, wait for God to assign people to help you and don't try to choose help on your own. The right people will have the faith to believe you will overcome what you are facing.

Be careful who you share your problems with. Every person you know is not the kind of person that would aid you in solving your situation. Some people are pessimistic. Some people are insensitive. Some people are worriers. Some people are empowering. Learning the difference between these types of people will make all the difference in how quickly you get through your current situation. Some people will lighten your burden, and others will make your burden heavier.

Nothing good has ever happened to pessimistic people. So they will tell you about all the people they know who died from the same condition that you have. They take joy in telling you that your problem is too great to overcome and what you are going through will be the end to any dream that you may have. They also say things like, your life will never get good again because theirs didn't. Some people will even compare their condition to yours and tell you that their illness is not as bad as yours is.

Insensitive people are the worst. If you are going through the loss of a loved one, they will tell you insensitive things like God picked another flower for His garden in heaven or you have been grieving long enough and you need to get over it. They will tell you that they are there for you and never call to check on you or come to visit you when your heart feels like it will never stop hurting. They may also make you feel worse by implying that you caused the problem you're facing. Or worse yet, they will offer you some help, but the way they help you make you feel small and devalued.

There is nothing like experiencing a loved one who is a worrier when you tell them that you have a problem, a crisis, or a serious situation! They will give you their stress and anxieties because they love you so much and because their natural posture is to fear the worst. They believe that your situation is too great to overcome. Therefore, don't share your crisis or difficult situation with anyone who is known for their worrying or for being insensitive or pessimistic. Your situation is difficult enough without their additional stresses and negativity.

CHOOSE YOUR WINNING TEAM

Your relationships can make a great difference when you are going through the hard places in your life. Don't isolate yourself from the people who love and care about you. Just having them with you will allow you to endure the problem or hardship a whole lot better. Their love and support will also help you to stay strong. Our friends and family know lots of people who have survived all types of horrific situations who can show you the best options to solve the problem that is keeping you up at night. However, only confide in people who are overcomers. Select people who are battle tested, which means that they have proven to be victorious in the hard and difficult places in their own lives. They will help you to win. They will be able to walk you through the difficulty you are facing because they have the right mindset, knowledge, ability, and experience to share insight and options with you that will allow you to successfully solve your problem or crisis.

Look for people who have faith to believe that you will survive the challenge you have. Their prayers and encouragement will keep you standing when you don't think you can. Remember, you are stronger with others than you are alone.

However, when your storm seems too much to bear, talk less to people and talk more to God in prayer. Talking constantly about your problem will discourage you and stop you from enjoying the other parts of your life. Keep the details under wraps. Don't give updates about your situation too often because you will begin to focus on the problem instead of the solution. It will also make your problem seem much bigger than it actually is.

Chapter Three:

BE MINDFUL OF YOUR ENVIRONMENT

What we think and what we say about our circumstances will make all the difference in whether we overcome them. However, we must be careful about what we feed our minds. It will determine what we believe about our situation. Therefore, be mindful about the things you watch and listen to. All of these things will influence the way you see the problem you are facing. Watching the news and television that show pictures of violence, hate, death, hopelessness, and despair will discourage you and make you believe that your problem is impossible to overcome.

My trust in God made me feed my faith with the word of God by listening to awesome sermons and lots of gospel music throughout the day. This kept me encouraged and allowed me to keep my spirit strong.

When those negative thoughts came into my mind, I was able to replace them with the promises of God. Learn to trust God no matter what things look like. God is able to do what you and no one else can do. Put your confidence in God! He is a sure bet! He has the power to change things and situations that seem impossible. He will work everything out in the end. Just believe and keep your faith in God. Don't allow yourself to believe the negative thoughts that will flood your mind. Replace those negative thoughts with the hope-filled promises of God's Word. Be sure to speak the Word of God in spite of what is going on in your life. Focus on what you want to happen not what you see. In the natural, it never looks good. That is why God's Word tells us to walk by faith and not by sight. Keep your faith in God's love for you, and He will surely bring you through the trial you are facing.

PRAISE YOUR WAY THROUGH YOUR PROBLEMS

When we are in a difficult place, we tend to complain about our problem and the things we don't have. We should take that same energy to thank God for what we do have and all the blessings He has already given us. This will allow God to move on our behalf because

God loves to be praised, and He also loves us to have a heart of gratitude. When our praise turns into worship, our problems become much smaller and easier to manage because we stop magnifying our problems and we start magnifying our God.

Chapter Four:

KEEP LIVING YOUR LIFE

Make the decision to live your life no matter what. Refuse to allow what you see to be what you believe. Your life is still worth living even though you are facing a problem or situation. Don't let your circumstances become your life. Continue to do the things you enjoy. Allow yourself to have fun. If going to the movie with friends bring you joy, then do it. If you have a hobby that you like, continue that hobby. Don't let your problem overshadow your life and what makes your life worth living.

BE SOMEONE ELSE'S BLESSING

Serve your way through your storm. Take the focus off of yourself and your problem by helping others who are going through a difficult time. Make a difference every day in some way. This will allow you to value your life, and the difference you make in the lives of others will give you fulfillment. Because I refused to be depressed or stressed, I made the decision to allow God to heal my body and walk me through every situation that I was facing and trust that He was working everything out for my benefit, and He did! During that most difficult time in my life, I was able to help some ladies who were going through some difficult situations by opening up my home for them to stay and giving them the support, love, and friendship they desperately needed. I was able to continue to having my Sister Circle Gatherings in my home which encouraged many women by giving them a safe, loving, and nurturing place to share their journey of womanhood. I also volunteered at a public library in an underprivileged neighborhood. I continued to enjoy my family, my friends, and the many strangers who came into my life during that time. Life with a problem is still a life worth living!

THERE ARE BLESSINGS IN THE MIDST OF YOUR CHALLENGE

You have the victory in spite of what your situation looks like! When you look around, you will soon discover that there are more good times to enjoy;

wonderful things to experience; amazing people to love and people to love you. Look at what I would have missed if I had not decided to enjoy my life in the midst of the challenges that I was facing. When I looked back on all the things that I experienced during those difficult years, there was a lot of joy and happiness in spite of what I was going through. I met wonderful people along the way who I would not have met if I didn't have those particular situations and circumstances. Some of the wonderful people I met made major differences in other areas of my life like speaking opportunities, and selling thousands of copies of my book, *Sister Circle: The Power of Sisterhood – A Guide to Becoming the Woman God Designed You to Be*. They also made my life more fulfilling and more enjoyable. I experienced some wonderful things from each of them. I was exposed to things I didn't even know existed. I met other people who understood things about life that I didn't understand. I was able to share some things with them that they didn't know as well. Let's face it, there will always be challenges in life. Life will never be perfect and without some type of situation, but life is still worth living! Especially when you decide that nothing is worth giving up on life for.

Chapter Five:

GOD WILL LEAD YOU

SEEK HELP FROM THE EXPERTS

Sometimes when life hits you, it hits with several things one right after another. I was already facing the foreclosure of my home. Then, I was sued by a collection agency. After that, I was diagnosed with skin cancer. If all of that wasn't enough, I was then diagnosed with breast cancer in my left breast. All I can say is if it had not been for the grace of God, all of these things would have been the end of me!

One of the greatest mistakes we can make when we are in the midst of a crisis or serious situation is to isolate ourselves from others, and not allow anyone to know what we are going through! When we keep our situations to ourselves, we become overwhelmed, and we convince ourselves that there is nothing that we can do to change what we are going through. Then, our minds get the best of us by telling us that others will judge us, or it is too embarrassing to let others know. When we let someone who cares for us know what we are going through, they help to make our problem so much lighter.

Because God is always guiding us when we are going through the challenges of life, He shows up in amazing ways. When I was sued by a collection agency, I remembered that I had a LegalShield Membership, so I called the law firm in my state and spoke to one of their attorneys. The attorney told me that they don't really want to take me to court. They want me to agree to a payment plan. The attorney asked me how much I could put down and when. Then he asked me how much I could pay each month until the balance was paid. I told the attorney that I could put down $150 by the twentieth of the following month and that I could make a monthly payment of $50 every month until the balance was paid. The attorney looked up the court case and found the name and telephone number for the attorney who was representing the collection agency. He called the attorney who was representing the collection agency with me on the phone. He told the collection agency's attorney that he was my attorney and that I was on the phone with him. My attorney told the other attorney about the payment arrangement that I was able to make, and the other attorney told my attorney that he would email him a document with the agreed terms. I should sign it and email it back the collection agency attorney. He stated that he would withdraw his lawsuit and I did not need to come to court. I was so relieved. If I didn't have that $24.95 a month LegalShield Membership, I would have had to find an attorney and pay all of those court fees, which I did not have the money for. God has a way of preparing us for problems that are somewhere down the road in our lives.

The skin cancer diagnosis was not a serious as I thought. The skin cancer treatment was very easy. All I had to do was take five minute-UV light treatments in my dermatologist's office for a few months and use a cream twice a day.

God has a way of looking out for us and ensuring that we are aware of what we need to know. You see, when my dermatologist found the skin cancer, he referred me to a cancer doctor to ensure that I didn't have cancer anywhere else in my body. The cancer doctor had me take a series of test and one of the tests showed something in my left breast. The cancer doctor then had me take a mammogram. The mammogram also showed something in my left breast. The cancer doctor had me take a biopsy, and they found a small cancerous mass in my left breast.

The skin cancer diagnosis saved my life. My dermatologist stated that he doesn't usually send his patients with skin cancer to a cancer doctor. I had just had a normal mammogram two months prior to them finding breast cancer. If God had not had the dermatologist to send me to the cancer doctor, the cancer could have spread and remained undetected. God is on top of everything that we go through.

Being diagnosed with breast cancer, and making all the decisions about how to get rid of it, is an experience you do not want to have alone! The best approach for my breast cancer healing process was to seek out women who have successfully overcome breast cancer. In my case, I had two girlfriends who had already been through their own breast cancer healing process. I also reached out to several breast cancer support groups and organizations. The support, guidance, love, resources, and understanding I received from them provided me with everything I needed to achieve my own breast cancer healing. They shared their journeys, theirs dos, their don'ts, their highs, their lows, along with resources that met a lot of the financial needs I had. But, most importantly, they shared their victories. I received the answers to all of my questions and concerns with love, care, and hope. I started my own journey of breast cancer healing with my victory team that consisted of a cancer doctor, a breast cancer surgeon, and nurses with more than twenty years of breast cancer healing success, and several women who had already had their own victory over breast cancer. Because of God and my awesome victory team, I had a stress and worry-free experience in spite of losing my left breast. God healed me from skin cancer, breast cancer, and He stopped me from being sued. The only thing left was the foreclosure of my home.

You see, when my house first went into foreclosure, I cried out to God to help me and show me what I needed to do. God had me to seek help and resources that knew all of the steps in the foreclosure process. This allowed me to stay calm and keep my emotions in check. They knew my rights, and they also knew the options I had at every step of the process. I decided not to keep my house because it cost more than it was worth and needed several thousand dollars of repairs. I got rid of my house debt and all of my other debt by filing bankruptcy, and I walked away with a clean slate. When we allow the experts to help us, things will always turn out better for us. I am so glad that I stayed hopeful and victory-minded. It kept me from becoming a victim and allowed me to keep fighting until God worked everything out.

Chapter Six:

OUR RELATIONSHIP WITH GOD IS OUR GREATEST ASSET

I f you want to get to the other side of a very hard place, the one thing that you must have is peace. True peace is what the Bible talks about in Philippians 4:7, "and the peace of God, which surpasses all understanding, will guard your hearts and minds through Christ Jesus." This kind of peace comes when you understand that God loves you, cares about you, and nothing happening to you is a surprise to God. In spite of what you are going through right now, God has an awesome plan for your life. The peace of God allows you to have some stability when the storms in your life are raging. It keeps the stress and worry from over-taking you.

When we know the God of our peace, we can rest in Him. We rest in God when we realize that He is in complete control of our lives, our circumstances, and everything else in the universe. If God wants us to do something, He will tell us what to do and will help us do it. Resting in God feels strange at first because it's not normal. We tell ourselves, "I must do something. I must try to figure something out. I must make something happen; I can't just sit still and do nothing." We want to see where the solution is coming from. We're not comfortable being in the "blind" and just trusting that God knows what's going on and how to work it out. The rest of God also allows us to get some much needed sleep for our body, our mind, our soul, and our spirit. When all of these areas are rested, we are better able to stay encouraged and stress-free and have the patience to wait on God to work out our situation.

However, we can't rest in God if we don't know Him. We know God when we have a personal relationship with Him for ourselves. God is our lifeline. He is the only one who can guide us safely through every challenge we will face in life. God's love heals us and makes us whole. Through His love, we are able to do all the work He has called us to do. Our strength, power, and wisdom come from God as we pray and seek Him for help. God is the only consistent help available to us twenty-four hours a day, and He allows us to come to Him just the way we are. God is the one who can tell us who He created us to be. He is the only one who has all knowledge about everything. He is the only one who can make the impossible possible. He has the power to work on our behalf and move the mountains we face. God loves you so much, and there is nothing that we can do to stop Him from loving us!

We start our relationship with God when we receive Jesus Christ as our Lord and Savior. Jesus gives us access to God the Father. According to the book of Romans in the Holy Bible, all of us have has sinned against God. Sin is anything against God's word, which is disobedience. The consequence of sin is death. If we die in sin, we will be eternally separated from God. Sin must be paid for before we can have a relationship with God. We cannot be good enough to pay for the sin we commit against God. Sin can only be paid for with the blood of someone who has not sinned, and that person is Jesus Christ. God gave his Son Jesus as a ransom to pay for the sins of everyone in the world because God loves us so much. The wages of sin is death, but the gift of God is eternal life in Christ Jesus, our Lord. Jesus is the only way we can get to Heaven. When we accept that Jesus died for us on the Cross, and He paid the price we owed to God for sinning against Him, we are saved and we become a part of the God's family.

You can receive the free gift of Salvation today by admitting you are a sinner. Understand that as a sinner, you deserve death. Believe Jesus Christ died on the Cross to save you from sin and death. Repent by turning from your old life to a new life in Jesus Christ. Receive through faith in Jesus Christ His free gift of Salvation.

Pray this prayer and you will start your personal relationship with God: *Dear Lord, I admit that I am a sinner. I have done many things that didn't please You. I have lived my life for myself. I am sorry and I repent. I ask You to forgive me. I believe that Jesus died on the Cross for me, to save me. You did what I could not do for myself. I come to You now. Take control of my life. I give my life to You. Help me to live every day in a way that pleases You. I love You, Lord, and I thank You that I will spend all eternity with You. Amen!*

If you accepted the Lord Jesus today, welcome to the family of God. Reach out to someone and tell them about your decision. Then locate a church that teaches God's Word, so you can grow and enjoy the life that God has just given you. Allow God to heal you and help you live the life that He has planned for you. Read your Bible daily. Meet together with other people who believe in Jesus. Get involved in a ministry group. Talk to God every day and enjoy your new life. According to 2 Corinthians 5:17, in the Holy Bible, you have a brand new beginning, "Therefore, if anyone is in Christ, he is a new creation; old things have passed away; behold, all things have become new."

Get ready for a life that you never dreamed possible! God bless you!

Chapter Seven:

LESSONS TO REMEMBER

T he ideal way to enjoy your life when you have a trial or tribulation is to have a life that you enjoy living before the problem shows up. You will have the stability you need to keep standing. A personal relationship with God will help you create that life. Nothing is ever as bad as it seems when we see things through the hope of God and His love for us. I heard is said that life is the greatest gift that God has given us and what we do with our life is our gift to God. Therefore, don't try to live your life without the help and guidance of God. There is too much to figure out with our limited mind and understanding. God has a wonderful plan for your life and only He can show you how to obtain it. His Love and forgiveness will heal you and allow you to live a life that you never dreamt possible. He will show you how to make right decisions and choices that will keep the negative things and people out of your life. But, most importantly, He will show you who you truly are and what He created you for. He will also help you to love and forgive yourself along with anyone who has hurt you. He will reveal the gifts and talents that He put in you and bring you before people who will value you for sharing those gifts and talents. He will also show you the truth about the lies that the Devil has been telling you about you and your life. He will help you break habits and strongholds that have kept you bound for years.

DON'T RESIST WHAT YOUR SITUATION IS CREATING IN YOU

My faith is now fortified. I got to know God in a deeper and much more personal way. I was able to trust God in ways I never had before. I learned how to include Him in every area of my life and depend on Him instead of myself. God became my Lord and not just my Savior! I let God sit in the driver's seat of my life instead of me. I started having quality time with God at the beginning of my day. When everything became too much to bear, I would pray to God and ask Him for more Grace to stay encouraged. I also cried my tears on God's shoulders instead of people. When I did, they were tears of thanksgiving and appreciation for what He had done and was doing to work out all of the things I was facing. During that time, I also learned how to better help other people who were going through difficult places in their lives. I also become a better friend because I was not weighing people down with my problems. I learned what the Bible says in Nehemiah. 8:10b (NJKV), "for this day is holy to our Lord. Do not sorrow, for the joy of the LORD is your strength."

I believed that life is what you make it, but we must decide what we want it to be. I have been living the life I want for the past six years. My relationship with God helped to know who I am in Him and what He created me to do. One thing He created me to do is to help people see themselves through the eyes of God's unconditional love for them, so they can be free to be their true selves. Today, I am cancer-free and I am living a brand new Chapter in my life that will be better, more enjoyable, and fulfilling than my life has ever been! Don't give up on your life when you are dealing with a difficult situation. As you can see, life does get good again and, most times, much better than it was. Remember, after you get the victory over what you are facing, become the guiding light for someone else's dark place by telling others what God did for you. This is how we give God the glory for the great things He has done.

SCRIPTURES THAT HELP ME REST IN GOD

I t was God's Word that gave me the strength and hope I needed to overcome every challenge I spoke about in this book. They reminded me about the promises of God that are available to me as a follower of Christ Jesus. They also allowed me to rest in His love for me. It is my hope that you will use the following scriptures to encourage you when you are going through the challenges of life!

(God Never Changes) Hebrews 13:8 (NKJV)

Jesus Christ *is* the same yesterday, today, and forever.

(God's Strength) Nehemiah 8:10 (NKJV)

Then he said to them, "Go your way, eat the fat, drink the sweet, and send portions to those for whom nothing is prepared; for *this* day *is* holy to our Lord. Do not sorrow, for the joy of the LORD is your strength."

(God's Plan) Jeremiah 29:11-13 (NKJV)

[11] For I know the thoughts that I think toward you, says the LORD, thoughts of peace and not of evil, to give you a future and a hope. [12] Then you will call upon Me and go and pray to Me, and I will listen to you. [13] And you will seek Me and find *Me,* when you search for Me with all your heart.

(God's Love) Romans 5:8 (NKJV)

But God demonstrates His own love toward us, in that while we were still sinners, Christ died for us.

(God's Love) Romans 8:38-39 (NKJV)

[38] For I am persuaded that neither death nor life, nor angels nor principalities nor powers, nor things present nor things to come, [39] nor height nor depth, nor any other created thing, shall be able to separate us from the love of God which is in Christ Jesus our Lord.

(Mercy) Lamentations 3:22-23 (NKJV)

[22] *Through* the LORD's mercies we are not consumed, Because His compassions fail not. [23] *They are* new every morning; Great *is* Your faithfulness.

(God is with us) Joshua 1:8-9 (NKJV)

[8] This Book of the Law shall not depart from your mouth, but you shall meditate in it day and night, that you may observe to do according to all that is written in it. For then you will make your way prosperous, and then you will have good success. [9] Have I not commanded you? Be strong and of good courage; do not be afraid, nor be dismayed, for the LORD your God *is* with you wherever you go."

(God is with you) Hebrews 13:5 (NKJV)

Let your conduct *be* without covetousness; *be* content with such things as you have. For He Himself has said, "I will never leave you nor forsake you."

(Help) Isaiah 41:10 (NKJV)

Fear not, for I *am* with you; Be not dismayed, for I *am* your God. I will strengthen you, Yes, I will help you, I will uphold you with My righteous right hand.

(Help) Psalm 121:1-3 (NKJV)

1 I will lift up my eyes to the hills From whence comes my help? 2 My help *comes* from the Lord, Who made heaven and earth. 3 He will not allow your foot to be moved; He who keeps you will not slumber.

(Help) 1 Peter 5:7 (NKJV)

Casting all your care upon Him, for He cares for you.

(Help) Psalm 34:17 (NKJV)

The righteous cry out, and the LORD hears, And delivers them out of all their troubles.

(Help) Psalm 46:1 (NKJV)

God *is* our refuge and strength, A very present help in trouble.

(Don't worry) Philippians 4:6 -7 (NKJV)

[6] Be anxious for nothing, but in everything by prayer and supplication, with thanksgiving, let your requests be made known to God; [7] and the peace of God, which surpasses all understanding, will guard your hearts and minds through Christ Jesus.

(Don't worry) 1 John 4:18 (NKJV)

There is no fear in love; but perfect love casts out fear, because fear involves torment. But he who fears has not been made perfect in love.

(Don't worry) Matthew 6:34 (NKJV)

Therefore do not worry about tomorrow, for tomorrow will worry about its own things. Sufficient for the day *is* its own trouble.

(Ask God) Matthew 21:22 (NKJV)

And whatever things you ask in prayer, believing, you will receive."

(Seek God) Luke 12:29-31 (NKJV)

[29] And do not seek what you should eat or what you should drink, nor have an anxious mind. [30] For all these things the nations of the world seek after, and your Father knows that you need these things. [31] But seek the kingdom of God, and all these things shall be added to you.

(Guidance) Psalm 31: 3 (NKJV)

For You *are* my rock and my fortress; Therefore, for Your name's sake, Lead me and guide me.

(Guidance) Psalm 32:8 (NKJV)

I will instruct you and teach you in the way you should go; I will guide you with My eye.

(Guidance) Isaiah 42:16 (NKJV)

I will bring the blind by a way they did not know; I will lead them in paths they have not known. I will make darkness light before them, And crooked places straight. These things I will do for them, And not forsake them.

(Guidance) Proverbs 3:5-6 (NKJV)

⁵Trust in the LORD with all your heart, And lean not on your own understanding; ⁶ In all your ways acknowledge Him, And He shall direct your paths.

(God's Power) John 15:5 (NKJV)

I am the vine, you are the branches. He who abides in Me, and I in him, bears much fruit; for without Me you can do nothing.

(God's Power) Luke 18:27 (NKJV)

But He said, "The things which are impossible with men are possible with God."

(No one will defeat you) Isaiah 54:17 (NKJV)

"No weapon formed against you shall prosper, And every tongue which rises against you in judgment You shall condemn. This is the heritage of the servants of the Lord, And their righteousness is from Me," Says the Lord.

(God is able) Ephesians 3:20 (NKJV)

Now to Him who is able to do exceedingly abundantly above all that we ask or think, according to the power that works in us.

(God will fix it) Romans 8:28 (NKJV)

And we know that all things work together for good to those who love God, to those who are the called according to *His* purpose.

(Give it to God) Proverbs 16:3 (NKJV)

Commit your works to the Lord, And your thoughts will be established.

(Strong mind) 2 Timothy 1:7 (NKJV)

For God has not given us a spirit of fear, but of power and of love and of a sound mind.

(Strength) Philippians 4:12-13 (NKJV)

12 I know how to be abased, and I know how to abound. Everywhere and in all things I have learned both to be full and to be hungry, both to abound and to suffer need. 13 I can do all things through Christ who strengthens me.

(Encouragement) 2 Corinthians 12:9a (NKJV)

And He said to me, "My grace is sufficient for you, for My strength is made perfect in weakness".

(Hope) Hebrews 11:1 (NKJV)

Now faith is the substance of things hoped for, the evidence of things not seen.

(Trust God) Hebrews 10:23 (NKJV)

Let us hold fast the confession of *our* hope without wavering, for He who promised is faithful.

(Provision) Philippians 4:19 (NKJV)

And my God shall supply all your need according to His riches in glory by Christ Jesus.

(Believe) Mark 11:24 (NKJV)

Therefore I say to you, whatever things you ask when you pray, believe that you receive *them,* and you will have *them*.

(Peace) Isaiah 26:3 (NKJV)

You will keep him in perfect peace, Whose mind is stayed on You, Because he trusts in You.

(Reassurance) John 14:27 (NKJV)

Peace I leave with you, My peace I give to you; not as the world gives do I give to you. Let not your heart be troubled, neither let it be afraid.

(Rest) Proverbs 3:24 (NKJV)

When you lie down, you will not be afraid; Yes, you will lie down and your sleep will be sweet.

(Rest) Psalm 4:8 (NKJV)

[8] I will both lie down in peace, and sleep; For You alone, O LORD, make me dwell in safety.

(We will overcome) Romans 8:37 (NKJV)

Yet in all these things we are more than conquerors through Him who loved us.

(Right standing) 2 Corinthians 5:21 (NKJV)

For He made Him who knew no sin *to be* sin for us, that we might become the righteousness of God in Him.

(New beginning) 2 Corinthians 5:17 (NKJV)

Therefore, if anyone *is* in Christ, *he is* a new creation; old things have passed away; behold, all things have become new.

(True rest) Matthew 11:28-30 (NKJV)

28 Come to Me, all you who labor and are heavy laden, and I will give you rest. 29 Take My yoke upon you and learn from Me, for I am gentle and lowly in heart, and you will find rest for your souls. 30 For My yoke is easy and My burden is light."

About the Author

*C**heryle T. Ricks** is the President, Founder & CEO of The Women Empowerment Circle, LLC. Further, she is a mother of four, the grandmother of seven, an Evangelist, a published author, a poet, a motivational speaker, and a former paralegal. She is a native Baltimorean who has lived in many different stations of life. She is an Alumna of Baltimore City Community College and Morgan State University.*

Cheryle has learned through her relationship with God that there is nothing that can disqualify anyone from having the life that Jesus Christ died for all of us to have. Motivated by the love of God, Cheryle shows people how to keep living and enjoying their lives when they are going through the trials of life. With a relationship with God, we can make it through anything!

I f you enjoyed reading this book, check out my first
book, *Sister Circle: The Power of Sisterhood – A
Guide to Becoming the Woman God Designed You to
Be* on my website below. You may also reach out to me
on the same website. Happy reading!

www.sisters-circle.com

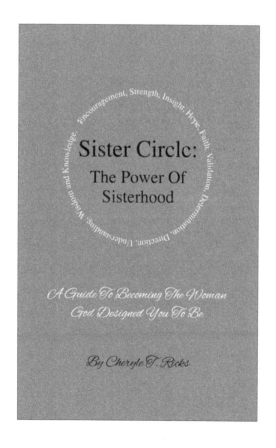